A Walk to the Store

By Judeah Reynolds
as told to Sheletta Brundidge
& Lily Coyle

Illustrated By
Darcy Bell-Myers

– BEAVER'S POND PRESS, SAINT PAUL –

Illustrated by Darcy Bell-Myers
ISBN: 978-1-64343-672-2
Library of Congress Control Number: 2022909550
First Printing: 2022

26 25 24 23 22   5 4 3 2 1

Cover and interior design
by Darcy Bell-Myers

Darcy Bell-Myers
Illustration & Design
www.bellmyers.com

SHElettaMakesMeLaugh.com

Beaver's Pond Press, Inc.
939 Seventh St. West
St Paul, MN 55102
(952) 829-8818
www.BeaversPondPress.com

To learn more about Judeah's journey,
visit: AWalkToTheStore.Com

For George Floyd

I'm too little to walk alone to the store.

So I ask everybody in the house, "Will you walk me to the store?"

"Will you walk me to the store?"

I have three dollars and I want to buy some candy.

But when we get to the store we see something bad. At first we don't know what's going on, but we know it's wrong. My cousin uses her phone to make a video.

We yell at them to **STOP**.

Other people yell too. We yell for a very long time. But it still *happens*.

We watch a man get killed.

We cannot stop it from happening. All we can do is tell what happened.

I cry and cry and tell my mom about it.

My cousin cries and tells about it. And she posts the video she made so other people can see how wrong it was.

Many people see the video. The next day a reporter comes to the door to ask about what happened.

More and more people learn about what we saw. They say that what happened was bad and wrong.

I keep thinking about it and feeling so sad. It is hard for me to sleep. When I sleep, I have bad dreams.

When I wake up from a scary dream, my mom gives me hugs. Hugs help me feel better.

I tell my mom I want to go back to the store. She's not sure that's a good idea, but I feel like I need to do it.

This time when I walk to the store, it doesn't look the same. I can see how many people care and want things to be better.

What we saw on our walk to the store was wrong. We knew it was wrong and we spoke up. Reporters, politicians, movie stars, churches, and schools are talking about it now. Many people are walking and protesting and writing letters and trying to make things change. They're working to make things better because we told what happened.

Even though some people do bad things, there are so many more people who want things to be good.

I'm too little to walk alone to the store.

But I'm big enough and brave enough to make things better in a very **BIG** way.

Sometimes bad things happen, but there are more good people than bad people. When something bad happens, tell it to the people you trust. Don't hold it inside.

How to Help Children Process a Traumatic Event

1. Help them feel safe. Children may have nightmares and worrisome thoughts of something bad happening again. Regularly remind them they are safe.

2. Remain regulated. Children reflect the emotions of the adults around them. Provide them with a calm, reliable adult presence.

3. Give them space to process. Allow children to share how they feel. They may want to talk about their feelings over and over again. Let them.

4. Limit their exposure to news coverage. Children may become overloaded and overwhelmed if they're repeatedly exposed to traumatic content.

5. Be open to differences in how children cope and process. Every child is different. Let them release and manage their trauma however they need to.

6. Try to keep things the same. A child who has experienced a disruptive traumatic incident needs normalcy and routine. Try to get back to their regular schedule.

7. Reassure children that the traumatic event is being addressed. Children may become consumed with not being able to control an outcome. Let them know it's being worked on.

8. Use real language. Don't downplay the traumatic event, dismiss it, or underestimate its impact. Use honest language that really speaks to the traumatic incident.

9. Give context to the situation. Share information and provide clarity about what actually happened in the traumatic event.

10. Get support if they continue to struggle. If your child is not functioning like they were before the traumatic event, or if things are not getting better, seek professional help.

–Anissa Keyes, MA, LMFT, LICSW
Arubah Emotional Health Services, PA
www.arubahemotionalhealth.com